RUDOLPH VALENTINO

DAY DREAMS

To M.

The serenade of a thousand years ago
The song of a hushed lip
Lives forever in the glass of today
Wherein we see the reflection of it
If we but brush away
The cobwebs of a douting faith.

Bibliografische Information der Deutschen Nationalbibliothek:
Die Deutsche Nationalbibliothek verzeichnet diese Publikation in der Deutschen
Nationalbibliografie; detaillierte bibliografische Daten sind im Internet über
http://dnb.dnb.de abrufbar.

© 2023 Matthias Adler-Drews (Herausgeber)

Herstellung und Verlag: BoD – Books on Demand, Norderstedt

ISBN: 978-3-7528-5111-3

RUDOLPH VALENTINO

DAY DREAMS

To J. C. N. G.

MY FRIENDS HERE AND THERE

INTRODUCTION

I can not tell a rondelay
In words of yesterday
I can not tell a couplet
For words come as they may.
I'll do my best — I'll try a bit
Of ultra-modern rhyme
And cast aside the shackles
Binding »Once upon a time«.

PREFACE

To you, my gentle reader, I wish to say a foreword
of warning before you peruse the contents of this book.
I am not a poet nor a scholar, therefore you shall find neither
poems nor prose. Just dreams — *Day Dreams* — a bit of
romance, a bit of sentimentalism, a bit of philosophy, not
studied, but acquired by constant observation of that greatest
of masters! . . . Nature!
While lying idle, not through choice, but because forcibly
kept from my preferred and actual field of activity, I took
to dreams to forget the tediousness of worldly strife and the
boredom of jurisprudence's pedantic etiquette.
Happy indeed I shall be if my Day Dreams will bring
you as much enjoyment in the reading as they brought to
me in the writing.

Rudolph Valentino

New York — May 29th, 1923.

THE GIFT BOOK
(To J. R.)

A book is a kindly gracious thing.
Each has a particular gift to bring.

It may be the wealth
      Of a wonderful life,
Or the thrilling adventure
      Of Jungle strife.
Perhaps it's a present
Of orient gold,
Tales of Aladdin
      Enchantingly told.
Maybe a view
      Of olden days,
Knighthood—Romance,
      Flowery ways.
And again a journey
      To lands afar,
Where strange things happen,
      And wonders are.

All of them—Gift books
      But plainly I see,

Not one of them holds
   The gift for me.
I want a book
   That will lazily roam
Down the dear Pathway
   To Folks back home.

NATURE

Nature is the open book
Wherein the truths of the world are found
Nature is an endless story
Of never changing glory
When you study nature your teacher is God
So always let your reference be
This Greatest of Masters.

THE LOVE CHILD
(To B.)

Don Juan roamed the summer sky
A shady cloud of gray
But this dull attire
Hid a heart of fire
In quest of romance stray.

Vision
A lovely golden sunbeam
Shining from above
Came radiant by
And caught the eye
Of this vagabond of love.

Delusion
In wild tempestuous wooing
He kissed her heart away
All in a jest
It was the quest
Of the cloud on a summer's day.

Conclusion
Through tears the sunbeam glimmered
Then happily she smiled
The tempest passed
Alone at last
With a little rainbow child.

Dawn runs in a crimson streak
        Across a leaden sky —
Just like a pulsing vein of life
An artery of love not strife
And it livens the heavens high.

So in our sky today it seems,
        No sign of life we see.
Do we not know,
Night's bound to go,
Dawn follows instantly.

If it were not for the showers, where
would the rainbows be?

HEART FLOWER

O lovely rose
      Within whose chalice lies
      The heart of my true love,
Did not the gods in benediction stoop
      To bless thee from above?
      And place within thy roseate lips
      The rubies counterpart.
      I found it there
      A jewel rare
The flower of thy heart.

YOU

Your Eyes
Your Eyes,
  Mystic pools
    Of beauteous light.
  Golden brown
    In color
      Deep,
        Yet, amber clear.
Unshadowed
  By a frown,
Fathomless,
  Wherein
    My senses
      Drown.
Your Eyes.

Your Lips
Your Lips,
  Twin silken petals
    Of a dewy rose.
  Altar
    Of the heart

Where love
  Kindling desire
    Worships unafraid.
  Crucible
    Of
      Passion.
  The rose in masquerade.
Your Lips.

  Your Kiss
Your Kiss,
  A flame
    Of Passion's fire
  The sensitive Seal
    Of Love
  In the desire,
    The fragrance
      Of your Caress;
  Alas,
    At times
      I find
        Exquisite bitterness
  In
Your Kiss.

DAY DREAMS
(To The Friend)

Yesterday — in contemplation
   We dreamed of love to be,
   And in the dreaming,
   Wove a tapestry of Love.

Today — We. dream our dream awake;
   Realization,
    Coloring our Romance
   With all the glory
    Of a flaming Rose.

Tomorrow — What awakening lies before us
   Our tapestry
    In shreds perchance,
   Or mellowed—glorified
    By love's reflection?

I wonder —

SUSPICION

There crossed the path
    Of my dream of you
A gossamer web of gray,
    So soft its sheen,
    Almost unseen,
But it stopped me
    On my way.

Like a cold, gray granite battlement
    It walled me all about,
For a cruel steel,
    Was in the feel
Of the silken web of doubt.

THE SAGE

(To M.)

O Gladness shining bravely
    From out the eyes of youth,
Be strong in your belief of good,
    Of valor and of truth.
For soon enough,
Too soon enough —
The gladdest light meets doubt,
Then flickers, flutters, just a bit,
    But, doesn't quite go out.

O Sadness peering divinely
    From out the eyes of age,
Be strong in your belief of good.
    To youth — still be the sage.
For soon enough,
Too soon enough,
The saddest light in doubt,
Flickers, flutters, flickers,
    And finally goes out.

MORPHIA

I am The Ingrate Morphia,
You hold the brimming cup of your Life
To me, athirst am I,
And drink my fill
Of strength, until
The cup is drained dry.

Then, satisfied, I care no more.
The cup, I cast away,
Crunch 'neath my heel.
Its doom I seal,
As I walk on my way.

DOMINO

Passion's cloak,
An ashy thing to wear,
Covering the shroud of love
That once was fair.

What gruesome imagery
Does this convey to me.
Grim death — itself no ghastlier a thing than this
Could ever be.

THE SPHINX
(To B. H.)

O Sphinx—a monument to man!
  Built by his hands of clay,
You symbolize the power of might
  Used in an earthy way.
Yesteryear, you stood for man's symbolic strength sublime,
  Today, you all but buried are
Beneath the sands of time.

O Wondrous mountain — living Sphinx!
  Built by the hand of God,
You symbolize the power of Love
  Used with the lowly sod.
Yesteryear, a symbol of divinity sublime,
  Today, you lift your rugged head
Untouched by hands of time.

O Sphinx — a monument to man!
  Built by his hand of clay,
You symbolize the power of might
  Used in an earthy way.

Yesterday, you in grandeur stood alone.
  Today, you're mingling with the sand
A rotting mass of stone.

O Wondrous mountain — living Sphinx!
  Built by the hand of God,
You symbolize the power of Love
  Used with the lowly sod,
E'er yesterday, you stood a monument of Love,
  Today unchanged, your glorious face,
    In worship turned above.

STRADIVARIUS
(To Jascha Heifetz)

If power were only given me,
To paint the tone picture that arises from the soul
Of that sanctuary of sound — your violin,
Where would I find pigment worthy of such a use,
Save in the fleeting splendour of some sky.
Where a brush — save in a snowy feather
From the shining wing of an archangel.
Where the canvas — save across the dream memory
  of one who heard
And was blessed by the hearing.

EXTRAVAGANZA

Extravaganza! The very word is vulgar. Still vulgarity is necessary to development, for even a weed growing in a swamp can sometimes be cultivated into a hot house plant. Take an orchid not under its own surroundings, but dress it by putting it in a proper receptacle, and what a difference! But, outside of beauty what have you? If we could only combine the beauty of an orchid with the soul of a weed we would get an improvement in the orchid, for real weeds are grateful enough to spring up between cobblestones, even to be trampled upon.

Rather be a blade of grass that knows the heart beats of Mother Earth, than the potted plant which is pampered and only restored to a semblance of life.

MIRAGE

Happiness—you wait for us
　Just beyond,
　　Just beyond.

We know not where,
　Nor how we shall find you.
We only know you are
　Waiting, waiting,
　　Just beyond.

GLORIFICATION
(To W. W.)

The arms of the earth broke through the sod
And clenched his fist in derision,
For clay knows not the might of God,
It has but earthy vision.

The finger of God wrote in the sky
A sign of mighty fire:
»Reach up to me for I am Life«
But earth could reach no higher.

With strength of muscle, with might and main,
Earth struggled and then defied,
But God stretched forth His hand of Love
And Earth was glorified.

REMEMBRANCE
(To M. O.)

An infant memory,
    A tiny fragile thing,
Called into being
    By the brush of a colored wing
Across the canvas
    Of my tired mind.
It grows,
    A lovely picture of the past I find,
You! Grown to fullest stature
    Of the perfect soul,
The tiny sheltered memory
    Has reached at last its goal.

THREE GENERATIONS OF KISSES

(To M. K.)

A Mother's kisses
Are blessed with love
Straight from the heart
Of Heaven above.
Love's Benediction,
Her dear caress,
The sum of all our happiness.

Till we kiss the lips
Of the mate of our soul
We never know Love
Has reached its goal.
Caress divine,
You reign until
A baby's kiss seems sweeter still.

That beloved blossom
A baby's face
Seems to be
Love's resting place.

And a million kisses
Tenderly
Linger there in ecstacy.

Were I told to select
Just one kiss a day;
Oh! What a puzzle
I would say.
Still a baby's kiss
I'd choose, you see,
For in that wise choice
I'd gain ALL Three.

A BABY'S SKIN

Texture of a butterfly's wing,
Colored like a dawned rose,
Whose perfume is the breath of God.
Such is the web wherein is held
The treasure of the treasure chest
The priceless gift — the Child of Love.

GRATITUDE
(To A. T.)

The oleander blooms for me,
In dawning splendrous beauty,
I planted it so tenderly,
And love has done its duty.

All in a garden of the earth,
All in a plot of ground,
Wherein I found no bit of worth,
The seed I planted in the ground.

Tiny seed almost unworthy
To be cherished for thy looks,
But deep within the heart of you
Was wisdom never found in books.

You are the spirit of the good,
The joy, the beauty of all things,
You are the melody of life — the song
That Mother Nature sings.

And so to that sweet lullaby
You, in your perfumed cradle, rest

Safe in the arms of Mother Earth,
Held closely to her loving breast.

Until one happy wondrous day
When love so tenderly drew nigh,
Lifted your tiny hand of green
And turned your face toward the sky.

The oleander blooms for me,
In dawning splendrous beauty,
I planted it so tenderly
And love has done its duty.

SHADOWS

Shadows — gray symbol of a broken faith.
We cling to hope — in hope we find
The symbol of a broken heart.
Shadows — gray bleak gossamer web
Of what once was woven 'round my heart.
We slink within thy domain — the land of shadows.
For still we hope,
But knowing always, that a broken faith can never be restored
To more than it was — a Shadow.

ACCUSATION

Out of a shadowed corner
Comes a phantom of the past,
    To confuse me
    And accuse me
For a vain iconoclast.
    To chide me
    And deride me
In a seething scornful blast.
    To cheat me
    And defeat me,
Conscience, crucifies at last.

EVEN SONG

I sing a song to the sapphire sky
That curtains a sleeping earth.
I sing a song to the stars on high
That mark a jewel's worth.

My feeble voice, so weak it sounds,
A puny earthy cry,
Yet when its echo comes to me,
Angelic voice in harmony,
I know it is not I.

It was belief that gave it wing,
That weakling voice of mine,
And carried it where angels sing
God's Melody Divine.

GYPSIES
(To R. B.)

Little gypsies of the city,
Little sparrows — more's the pity,
Homeless, heedless of the weather,
Happy, banding all together,
Never giving thought to trouble,
Never seeing evil double,
Would that we who proudly mention
Every honorable intention
To the world with trumpet blaring,
Could, like sparrows, take uncaring
All the little earthly struggles,
Cast them gypsy-like aside
And fly happily, and gladly
All about earth's countryside.

Why do the birds chant the psalm of glory?
Only because they alone are free throated and unafraid.
Do they realize the danger in the sling-shot of
civilization? No — they are only conscious of the Joy
within.

Why sing of Joy —
　　If Joy is to be unheard.
Why sing of Faith,
　　If Faith is to be barred.
For all that is good
　　Is forever alive,
And all that is bad
　　Is dead before it be born.

THE CARRIER
(To J. K.)

A poor little messenger clad in gray,
Sent as a go-between — they say.
Took a betrayal under its wing
And guarded and cherished the slimy thing.

We speak of Glory, and Trust, and Men,
But that is all forgotten when
We send this softly feathered bird
With messages best left unheard.

Oh! What a mockery 'cross the sky
The dove is sent to act as spy.

THE SCHOOL OF LIFE
(To M.)

Lives are classes — we are pupils with excellent teachers. Experience should tutor us, but we so often shirk school. School can be made happy and we delight in making a higher grade — but through not heeding Experience's teaching we often are left back in the old class, and sometimes, sad to relate, are put several grades lower.

But, happily, there is always the opportunity of skipping many grades upward. It's a poor rule that doesn't work both ways.

The Mind is the Grade we work in. We can have majestic thoughts, living in a hermit's hut, or we can think as a swine in a palace on a throne of gold — let us choose our station — kingly children, or swineherds. Eternity is the Empire.

THE WANTON

To love, save that which mockery was
No heart, save that of stone.
A multitude forever hers,
Alas — not one — alone!

Cradled in the arms of many,
Not where to lay her weary head.
Fortune smiled — held out her hand
And struck the wanton dead.

SLAVERY
(To E. A. P.)

Love
I am a slave,
Yet free as birds above,
Sold into bondage
By the tender kiss of love.

Lust
I am a slave
In the rat trap of disgust,
Sold into bondage
By the lurid kiss of lust.

Hate
I am a slave
Prisoned by the walls of fate,
Sold into bondage
By the cruel kiss of hate.

Crime

I am a slave
Behind the bars of time,
Sold into bondage
By the leprous kiss of crime.

Death

I am a slave
No longer in my breath.
Given sight of freedom
Through the graciousness of death.
Still am I a slave
In the hand of destiny,
Thought alone enslaved me
And thought alone can free.

WITHIN A WALL

Once in a time when skies were gray
I chanced to walk in a cloistered way,
I saw the ones who closed the door
On all the world had spread before.
Their eyes — that were closed to the joy of good,
They thought the God's law they understood.
O Pity, Pity, for such as they
Who only look on skies of gray,
From cloistered windows sad of eye,
When all about is glorious sky.
It was but the tiny patch of gray,
The shadowed thing that happened to play
Behind the back of the glorious earth.
Alas, they thought it was all the worth
Of the whole wide world, the glorious world.
But the folded wings were not unfurled
And closed to use they lost the call,
And so they lost to them their all.

THE CHALICE
(To E. H.)

The chalice of a lily cup
Is indeed the sacrament
That Mother Nature uses
When she communes with God.

SOLICITUDE

On the sands of a happy shore,
Walked two lovers, hand in hand,
Leaving all that's gone before.
They mark each footstep in the sand,
Knowing well that every foot print
Will be trod by their own blood,
Therefore, let each couple ponder
O'er their footsteps
For future good.

(To D. K.)

Man is the word of the story,
Woman is the inspiration,
God is the book that binds,
None other can be what is now the finished book.

YOU

You are the History of Love and its Justification.
The Symbol of Devotion.
The Blessedness of Womanhood.
The Incentive of Chivalry.
The Reality of Ideals.
The Verity of Joy.
Idolatry's Defense.
The Proof of Goodness.
The Power of Gentleness.
Beauty's Acknowledgment.
Vanity's Excuse.
The Promise of Truth.
The Melody of Life.
The Caress of Romance.
The Dream of Desire.
The Sympathy of Understanding.
My Heart's Home.
The Proof of Faith.
Sanctuary of my Soul.
My Belief of Heaven.
Eternity of all Happiness.
    My Prayers.
      You.

AT SUNRISE TOMORROW
(To E. B.)

O Love, when you leave me do not say:
»Tomorrow we meet at twilight.«
For that is the time of the darkening hour,
The ending of the day.
All is glowing, gleaming in our love,
All is pulsing, breathing in the light
Of understanding — it is not symbolic of twilight,
Nor yet of dawning, for it has reached the zenith of love's day.
So when you leave me, dearest, do not say:
»Tomorrow we meet at twilight.«
Rather, beloved of my heart,
»We meet at sunshine tomorrow.«

POVERTY

Possessing the jewels of the earth,
Holding within my grasp the sceptre of the universe,
All these would but make me more the pauper —
Were I beggared of your love.

CREMATION
(To G. S.)

I

Just a packet of letters tied with a bit of blue,
Just a packet of letters that once were sent by you
To one who proved unworthy
Of the Love inscribed within.
The tiny packet of letters, a witness of my sin.

II

Just a packet of letters, but they are not mine own.
I dare not claim one thought in them
Not even as a loan,
For to the one you thought I was
In all sincerity
You bared the secrets of your soul.
Now I send them back to thee.

Ill

Just a packet of letters
A monument of love.
You lie within the fireplace,
In smoke you'll rise above
The sordidness of all deceit,
The grime of earthly thought,

Yet, in this flash of living fire,
The flame of love is caught.

IV

Just a packet of letters a while ago you were,
Now in vaprous symphony of gray
I send you back to her,
For the spirit of true love that's penned,
Must rise to meet her soul
In pearly glory 'round her head.
Love's halo — is its goal.

To rake over the dead ashes of a burnt out love one must use the pen point of poetry.

THE LUTE

The lute, a barrier to song of soul.
    For none save God
    Can music charm
From out a thing man-made.
    A bowl of wood,
    A string or two to arm
The troubadour with weapon strong.

POWERLESS

When I see a look of sadness,
   In the eyes of You,
Thoughts of grief akin to madness
   Surge my being through.

Am I then so weak and helpless,
   That I can not send
Even shadowings of sorrows
   To their deserved end.

Garden of delight wherein the jewels of earth do lie!
Tell me, in your vault of gold, will the flowers ever die?
Nothing of so fair a mien could return to earthly dust.
Even if the earth do say, »It is finished«, trust we must
In the God who tells of light that will lift to Heaven above
Every perfumed flower that blows symphonies on wings of love.

CAP AND BELLS
(To F.)

In Life's masquerade the disguises are many:
Here's a man masquerading as Wealth,
Wears a million of gold,
But a pauper, I'm told,
He hasn't a penny of health.

Here comes a Beggar, in tatters and rags,
Masking as Poverty old.
He may look the part,
But the wealth in his heart,
Makes him richer than Croesus in gold.

The costumes are varied disguises beguiling
That cover the true man beneath
One wears learned looks,
That he's borrowed from books
And a co-operative laurel wreath.

And still another pretending a clown,
In make-up the silliest Fool,
But his knowledge of men,

Is beyond the ken
Of a sage of the orthodox school.

There are millions of others in Life's Motley Masque
Who follow the art of mime.
They mimic and play
At mockery today,
But they never fool Old Father Time.

PATCHWORK QUILT

A Patchwork Quilt,
Industrious name.
Once it was not quite the same.
A different fame,
A »Crazy Quilt«,
Same foolish dame
Entitled you.
It was sorry fame.
Life is like that,
We do not see
How little bits
Make harmony —
It's up to man to take each bit
Of happiness and make it fit.
But if he takes and doesn't dwell
Upon the pattern — Well, it's Hell!
A crazy quilt the name's O. K.
But start a patchwork quilt today.

To A. M.

The sky is the mirror that reflects all phases of Life. The clouds of Doubt bring showers, but there is always the »Silver Lining« promise.

Moral: If the sky is the limit better fix it clear in your mind to begin with.

THE PHILOSOPHY OF A PESSIMIST

I do not care for money made easily,
It is not lasting — I know.
I do not care for friends made easily,
They are not lasting — I know.
I do not care for anything that comes easily,
It never lasts — I know.
But I fell in love with you easily,
But, not lastingly — I know.

GEMS OF THOUGHT

Diamonds — Scintillating wit of sharpest ray
Emeralds — Philosophy, growth in words today
Pearls — Are the hymns of pity
Sapphires — Songs of the skies
Rubies — Are poems of passion
And love that never dies.

To C. F.

The curtain is raised on the first act — the overture
is over. We can play our parts. They say
life's a stage, but what a sad thing we have so few
good stage managers. Our productions have more
in the way of Costume and lack, so often, the right
lines. Lines do count, not always words, but sympathy
of thought is quite as necessary.

SYMPATHY
(To J.)

Sympathy is just as essential to the world as any
other great attribute of good, but it must be sympathy
in the right place.

Sympathy of thought has been the greatest lever
in the machinery of mankind, but to sympathize
with a weak nature sometimes breaks up his foundation.
Know your subject.

Never withhold sympathy in loving one, but
rather than sympathy, use encouragement as a tonic
to tone up a weakling.

Kindly sympathetic interest is only another name
for encouragement.

Never take away a prop without putting a
stronger one in its place.

On a stretch of sandy beach I see naught of human
presence, but upon looking closer, a remembrance
of the past. I sit upon a rock and meditate

upon what once was. I see myself in all the splendor
of my youth. I see my boon companion —
Hope, and one other one, whose name I'd best
forget. We walked — Hope and I — but ever the
unnamed one stalked by my side. I turned to gaze
in fascination at my companion who speaks not, but
forever stalks silently beside me. I finally forget my
Hope to gaze in interest at the other. Hope, neglected,
lags behind until we walk alone — myself
and the unnamed one. We walk forever, but the
walk brings us to the abyss of the world. What
name has that one whose identity I fail to know?
O, Eternity, thou art my sight and knowledge. It
was Doubt, whose companion I became.

LABOR

On whose shoulders are the crosses held,
None can liken a laborer to him who bears the heavy-hearted thoughts.
What can I say — it is more laborious than many tasks,
Yet — 't is not task —
For task is given to be done
And ye are the cross bearers if ye will.

WEALTH

(To B. F. S.)

Treasures in the lowly casket that we call a brain,
Can jewels of the earth compare
With all that man finds hidden there?

The wealth of knowledge, that will lead a willing soul
Into a land of untold wonder,
Where will be the lasting goal
Of every seeking thought —

UNDERSTANDING
(To the Brother of Maris)

Maris of the golden eyes,
    You in all innocence
Looked upon a lovely world
    In wondering shyness.
Beauty beckoned,
    Then turned the corner of another day
Leaving in her stead
    An unknown one,
The stranger to light.

Maris of the saddened eyes,
    In your pity,
Looking from another world
    Have compassion on beauty
Who thoughtlessly turned away,
    Leaving another in her place
The stranger to light.

HUNGER

I have journeyed toward the city
On the long, long road of Life,
I have learned how little Pity
Plays a speaking part in life.

I have learned that only Money
Is the voice that's heard today,
Calling for God's milk and honey,
Even Hunger has no say.

I have reached the city's center
By the crooked road of Hell,
For Starvation's been my mentor
And has taught her lesson well.

MONEY

Money — you Harlequin of the great masquerade of life.
You wear the dollar sign as your mask.
It may hide you — yes, for a time,
But when at last grim reality stalks into the midst of the
    festivities,
The mask is ruthlessly torn away, and then — is seen
The true expression hidden behind it — the cruel visage of
    discordant greed.

THE CHOICE

Words are jewels rare —
  If need be
Words are sometimes fair
  You heed me,
But our choosing makes them seem
The reflection of a dream.

Let us, therefore,
  Choose in reason,
Whereby all that good is ours,
And by knowing rightful season
Pass forever — happy hours.

ITALY
(To Caruso)

The earth is earth — that is its worth,
To men who walk below.
But to the soul that seeks its goal,
Each land is all they know.
One calls it Home, another Heart, another Property,
But to the one who loves the sun
He calls it Italy.

ERIN

The green sod is red now —
    Rebellion
The green sod is white now —
    Purity
The green sod is blue now,
    With truth
And the green sod is ever green,
    It is growth — none can stop natural growth
Erin — land of dreams — Awaken.

BEES

The air is alive with buzzing bees
The little workers of destinies.
We grasp and strive to make our way,
Each life a hive and so our day
Is fraught with honey sweet, if we
Know all is good in destiny.

To M. T.

A certain lad had a long way to go, so he sat
still and waited until — well, another lad also had
a long way to go — so he hurried along and before
long he received several gifts not to be sneezed at.
No, they were not to be sneezed at, though I must
say they made his eyes water a bit. The gifts were
lovely little blisters on his pedal extremities, so he
had to sit down and take care of his poor feet and
in pain tarried, looking at his poor feet. Ah, yes,
our other little lad took it very slowly, almost like
the proverbial snail, but kept on the lookout and
pretty soon a nice, comfortable wagon came along,
and took the slow little boy for a nice ride, and the
good little slow boy rode merrily by the poor little
fast boy, who still sat nursing his blisters. He had
really gone stepping on some little brimstones, —
though he said they were pebbles. The good little
slow boy turned back and put his hand to the poor
little fast boy, but I regret to say he raised his digits
to his nose — O, world where is thy sting.

Note — This is not a moral, it is only something
that happens every day on our best trafficked roads.

IMPERIALISM

Oh, Mirror — most ungrateful ruler
    Man has ever had.
We trembling bow to your decree,
    But oh! 'T is very sad
For all our great devotion
    And concern in your behalf,
No matter how we worship you,
    You just give us the laugh.

Though we may claim democracy,
    You hold us like a slave.
The tyrant ruler of the world,
    From cradle to the grave.
Pa Adam's prize Apollos
    Look to you (It is to laugh)
Their reward for faithful service,
    Is Methuselah's Epitaph.

RADIO
(To H. M.)

Radio of romance,
      You
Broadcasting to the universe
      All that is most blessed
      In all things,
But to me alone
      The melody of your Love
    Flows through
      The artery
      Of time and Space,
For unity,
      Can never know Division.

THE KALEIDOSCOPE OF LOVE

Synonyms and Antonyms

A — Adoration — Anticipation — Affinity — Arguments.
B — Beauty — Bliss — Bitterness — Bondage.
C — Caresses — Circumstances — Confidences — Charm.
D — Desire — Delusion — Dreams — Divorce.
E — Ecstacy — Engagement — Ego — End.
F — Fascination — Forgetfulness — Flattery — Faith.
G — Gossip — Gratitude — Gift — Goodbye.
H — Happiness — Honor — Heartache — Hell.
I — Intuition — Irony — Idolatry — Integrity.
J — Jealousy — Joy — Justice — June.
K — Kisses — Keepsakes — Knowledge — Kismet.
L — Lips — Loneliness — Logic — Longing.
M — Marriage — Morality — Money — Man.
N — No — Nearest — Novelty — Never.
O — Opposition — Own — Offering — Opulence.
P — Passion — Promise — Pride — Proposal.
Q — Quality — Quest — Queries — Quarrels.
R — Romance — Reveries — Realization — Remembrance.
S — Sympathy — Sacrifice — Shame — Settlement.
T — Thoughts — Truth — Temper — Tears.
U — Unkindness — Understanding — Uncertainty — Unfaithfulness.
V — Virtue — Vanity — Vows — Vengeance.

W — Wisdom — Wishes — Wedlock — Woman.

X — The Unknown — Love.

Y — Youth — Yearning — Yes — Yawn.

Z — Zenith — Zest — Zeal — Zero.

MEMORIAL
(To A. S. R.)

A Saint in a stained glass window,
To the memory of one
Who »lived the life«,
In sin and strife,
Is the epitome of fun.

A bit of colored crockery,
A picture wrought in glass,
His memory's mockery
'T is best to let it pass.

A Saint in a stained glass window,
A blest memorial true,
When it reflects the beauty of
The memory of you.

DUST TO DUST

I take a bone — I gaze at it in wonder — You, O
bit of strength that was. In you today I see the
whited sepulchre of nothingness — but you were the
shaft that held the wagon of Life. Your strength
held together the vehicle of Man until God called
and the Soul answered.

LULLABY TREE

Cradle a thought on a bough of a tree,
Where it will swing so lazily,
Where it will gather to its heart
All in Nature's lovely mart.
For every lovely living thing
Stops to talk by a tree and sing,
Of what has gone on that very day
In fields and forests far away.

If little thoughts hear happily
All that's said about a tree,
They'll grow to be so wise and true,
They'll come back to the heart of you
Much stronger, grown in beauty free,
Because their cradle was a tree.

ADAGE

Happy childhood knows no sting
That the age of stealth doth bring.
Stealing hours from the day
Takes the joys of strength away.
Stealing hours from the Night
Taking all — for rest is Might.
When we steal away a Trust,
Nothing ever can we give
Back to him and so we must
Never Steal, but Give to Live.

FAITHFULNESS
(To Our Little Friend — The Dog)

A dog is the nearest approach to the sweet submissive
spirit God would have in us, Faithfulness in
the highest form. He only is faithful because he
believes in you, as God would have us believe in Him.

REFLECTIONS AT RANDOM

(To A. T.)

Sing a song to the moon
Or sing a song to the sun
But just as long as you sing a song
Your day or night is well begun.

Woman, the unreasonable Reason for the Great Reason,
   which the sages call Life — Others not so knowing call
   it Love.

Faith — The Engagement — repartee of Love.
Hope — Marriage — maybe its reply, but
Charity — Divorce — is the retort courteous.

The wedding march or two-step, I should say, is only too
   often the lock-step.

Punishment is seldom unmerited, though we may not always
   see the cause.

It is unwise to doubt others when you are not sure of yourself.

Scientists are fools in some respects, I mean the so-called ones, for they ignore the science of all important things.

Friend is symbolical of Heaven, but some play Hell with it.

Fun is a healthy disease and is very contagious.

»May I intrude« is often substituted for »Do I intrude« — bores are not connoisseurs in the selection of verbs.

Make the best of what comes, for the best is coming.

The Great Divide is the division of thought which separates the Wise from the Fools.

Whatever has in it the element of restlessness is like the poison ivy plant; it causes rash and spasmodic movements, and after all the scratching the victim is worse off than before.

Worlds, and Worlds to live in, and so few do.

Care is helpful if we carefully care, but when we carelessly care, be careful.

Gossip — never related in the same way.
When you eat hash you do not always recognize the different
kinds of meat in it, do you? So it is with Twice Told Tales.

We always prefer the most difficult way. It seems so much
more important, but once we realize it, truth is always
simplest when it is Truth.

It takes a hero to accuse no one, but take another's accusation
to his heart.

Love's greatest expression is Service.

Eyes are living windows.

Into the garden we all go, but most are looking for the worm
in the bud and never see the promise of the flower.

    ART the very mockery of it
    In a painted mask we sometimes call a face,
    Alas, that pigment be so badly used
    And artistry brought to much sad disgrace.

Take freedom but take care lest it take your liberty from you.

To be a humorist one must be concise, witty, but short-lived,
    for the good die young.

> Cleverness — word most useful to the Bard
> Who finds his pathway all beset with doubt,
> For if we find his hidden meanings hard,
> We call him »clever« — then he knows what we're about.

Publicity is the keystone in the Arch of Triumph.

Money—pretender to the throne of all we most desire.

Doubt is the opposing influence of our lives.

Happiness, some never know as a lasting friend, but only as
    a bowing acquaintance.

Wifehood is a profession, but Womanhood is the Expression.

Faith is the oasis in our Desert of Lost Hope.

Given a chance to run in the Great Race, even a weakling
can win if he wears the Armor of Courage.

Purpose in doing is the cornerstone of success.

Did anything ever build itself over night that was worthy
the name Great Structure?

Loving service is more helpful than scholarly advice.

Friend—Most lovely word, akin to love, its dearest relation —might I say.

We dream of Greatness in humility, only to awaken to the
greatness of Humility.

CO-OPERATION

O Just and Mighty Army of the World of Living Things
March on into the open heart of Man,
He needs a touch of nature with the sympathy it brings
In order to work out Life's Perfect Plan.

CONTENTS

CONTENTS